TEXAS
WRITE SOURCE

SkillsBook

Grade 2

GREAT
SOURCE®

HOUGHTON MIFFLIN HARCOURT

P9-CRX-578

A Few Words About the
Texas Write Source SkillsBook Grade 2

Before you begin . . .

The *SkillsBook* provides you with opportunities to practice editing and proofreading skills presented in the Student Edition of *Texas Write Source*. *Texas Write Source* contains guidelines, examples, and models to help you complete your work in the *SkillsBook*.

Each *SkillsBook* activity includes a brief introduction to the topic and examples showing how to complete that activity. You will be directed to the page numbers in the Student Edition of *Texas Write Source* for additional information and examples.

The "Proofreading Activities" focus on punctuation, capitalization, spelling, and usage. The "Sentence Activities" help you understand sentences and common sentence problems. The "Language Activities" highlight the parts of speech.

Many exercises end with a **KEEP GOING** activity. Its purpose is to provide follow-up work that will help you apply what you have learned in your own writing.

Printed in the U.S.A.

ISBN-13 978-0-547-39558-6

7 8 9 10 11 12 13 0928 16 15 14 13

4500414260   B C D E F G

Table of Contents

Proofreading Activities

Checking Mechanics

Using the Right Word

Sentence Activities

Language Activities

Proofreading Activities

The activities in this section include sentences that need to be checked for mechanics or usage. Most of the activities also include helpful references in the Student Edition of *Texas Write Source*. In addition, KEEP GOING, which is at the end of many activities, encourages follow-up practice of certain skills.

TEKS 2.22C(i)
ELPS 2C, 4C

Name

_____

Periods as End Punctuation

A **period** is used as a signal to stop at the end of a sentence. Put a period at the end of a telling sentence.

A **Put periods at the ends of these telling sentences.**

1. Our class lines up at the main door ___•___

2. Sometimes we make our teacher smile _____

3. We play indoors on rainy days _____

4. There are some great new books in the library _____

5. I like to write funny stories _____

B **Write two telling sentences about your school.**

1. _____

_____

2. _____

_____

★ TEKS 2.22C(i)

C **Put a period at the end of each sentence in this letter.**

> October 10, 2011
>
> Dear Aunt Fran,
>
>   I like school this year There are 22 kids in my class A new boy sits next to me His name is Robert I think we're going to be friends I'll let you know in my next letter
>
> > Love,
> >
> > Timmy

Now answer these questions about the letter.

1. How many telling sentences are in the letter? _____

2. How many periods are in the letter? _____

Name _____

Periods After Abbreviations

Use **periods** after these abbreviations:
Mr., Mrs., Ms., and Dr.

Dr. Green   Mrs. Linn

(**Dr.** is the abbreviation for **doctor**.)

A Put periods after the abbreviations in these sentences. (Some sentences need more than one period.)

1. Mrs. Linn is our teacher.

2. Mr and Mrs Linn have three rabbits.

3. Mr Linn gave the rabbits their names.

4. They are Ms Hop, Mr Skip, and Mrs Jump.

5. Mrs Linn took the rabbits to Dr Green for shots.

6. Dr Green said, "Those are good names!"

7. Mrs Linn told Dr Green that Mr Linn made up
   the names.

6

 Write two names for rabbits. One name should start with Mr. and one with Mrs. Then write two sentences that use the names.

Name: ___Mr._____

Name: ___Mrs._____

1. _____

_____

_____

2. _____

_____

_____

C **Write the names of four grown-ups. Be sure to write Mr., Mrs., Ms., or Dr. before each name.**

1. _____

2. _____

3. _____

4. _____

 **TEKS** 2.22C(i)
ELPS 2C, 3C, 4C

Name _____

Question Marks

Put a **question mark** after a sentence that asks a question.

What is the longest river?◄

A Put a question mark after each sentence that asks a question. Put a period after each of the other sentences.

1. The world's longest river is the Nile _____

2. Where is the Nile _____

3. The Nile River is in Africa _____

4. Are there crocodiles in the Nile _____

5. You could jump in and find out _____

6. Are you kidding _____

7. I'd rather just ask someone _____

8. Are you afraid of crocodiles _____

9. Who wouldn't be afraid _____

 TEKS 2.22C(i)

B Put a period or a question mark at the end of each sentence in this paragraph.

Lots of animals live in rivers Of course, fish live in rivers What else lives in rivers Snails, frogs, and turtles live in and around rivers Have you heard of river otters They are very good at diving They can stay underwater for four minutes Do you know any other animals that live in rivers

Write two questions about rivers. Remember to use question marks!

1. _____

_____

2. _____

_____

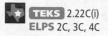 **TEKS** 2.22C(i)
ELPS 2C, 3C, 4C

Name _____

Exclamation Points

Put an **exclamation point** after an *excited* word. Also put an exclamation point after a sentence showing strong feeling.

Help! ←   Yikes!

Don't touch that! ←

A Use an exclamation point or period to finish each sentence. Remember, an exclamation point is used after each *excited* word and after each sentence that shows strong feeling. Telling sentences need a period.

1. I found a treasure map___!___

2. It was in my closet_____

3. I found the map when I cleaned my room_____

4. Wow_____

5. Let's find the treasure_____

6. We should ask our parents before we look_____

7. This could be fun_____

★ TEKS 2.22C(i)

B Each of the following sentences needs an exclamation point or a question mark. Put the correct end punctuation after each sentence.

1. Look, Tom, it's a cave _____

2. It's dark _____

3. It's creepy _____

4. Did you see that _____

5. What is it _____

6. It's a bat _____

7. Wow, that's neat _____

8. Here we go _____

Imagine that you are in a dark cave. Write a sentence that ends with an exclamation point.

_____

_____

TEKS 2.22C(i)
ELPS 2C, 3C, 4C

Name _____

End Punctuation

Use a **period (.)** after a telling sentence. Use a **question mark (?)** after a sentence that asks a question. Use an **exclamation point (!)** after a sentence that shows strong feeling.

 **Put the correct end punctuation after each sentence.**

1. Dad's taking us to the zoo __!__

2. Hooray! Let's have a race to the car _____

3. What animal does Dad like _____

4. He likes the elephants _____

5. What do you think Mom wants to see _____

6. She'll probably watch the giraffes _____

7. What should we do _____

8. Let's go see the seals _____

TEKS 2.22C(i)
ELPS 2G, 2H, 2I, 3C, 3E

 **Write a telling sentence, an asking sentence, and a sentence showing strong feeling about your favorite dinner.**

Telling Sentence: _____

_____

Asking Sentence: _____

_____

Strong Feeling Sentence: _____

_____

C **Ask a partner a question. Write your partner's name, the question you asked, and your partner's answer.**

Partner's Name: _____

Question: _____

_____

Answer: _____

_____

TEKS 2.22C(i)
ELPS 2C, 3C, 4C

Name _____

End Punctuation Review

Use a **period** after a telling sentence. Use a **question mark** after a sentence that asks a question. Use an **exclamation point** after a sentence that shows strong feeling.

A **Put the correct end punctuation after each sentence.**

Does this ever happen to you It's time for bed, but you're not sleepy You try to lie still You look around You just have to get up You want to get a book or a toy You try to be quiet It's hard to see in the dark You make a loud noise Someone says, "What's going on in there" Then you hear, "Get back in bed"

TEKS 2.22C(i)

 **Draw a picture of something you like to do after school.**

 **Write three sentences about your picture. First write a telling sentence. Next write a question. Then write a sentence that shows strong feeling.**

1. Telling Sentence:_____

_____

2. Asking Sentence:_____

_____

3. Strong Feeling Sentence:_____

_____

ELPS 2C, 4C

Name _____

Commas Between Words in a Series

Put **commas** between words in a series.

The five senses are sight, hearing, taste, smell, and touch.

A Put commas where they are needed in these sentences.

1. Most foods taste sweet, sour, or salty.

2. Smell sight and taste help us enjoy food.

3. Almost everybody likes warm bread biscuits and dinner rolls.

4. Lilies lilacs and roses smell good.

5. Cats can see only black white and gray.

6. Dogs cats and bats hear all kinds of sounds.

7. Sounds can be loud soft or just right.

8. Teddy bears are soft cuddly and fuzzy.

ELPS 5F

List three or four things in each category below.

My Favorite **Tastes**	My Favorite **Smells**	My Favorite **Sounds**

Finish the sentences below using words from your lists. Remember to use commas between words in a series.

1. My favorite tastes are _____

_____ and _____ .

2. My favorite smells are _____

_____ and _____ .

3. My favorite sounds are _____

_____ and _____ .

ELPS 2C, 4C, 5F

Name _____

Commas in Compound Sentences

A **compound sentence** is two short sentences connected by **or**, **and**, or **but**. Always use a **comma** before the connecting word.

I have a goldfish, and I feed it once a day.

A Add a comma to each of these compound sentences.

1. I love hamburgers, but I do not like onions.

2. My brother is three and he goes to preschool.

3. You can walk or you can ride your bike.

4. Dad came to the concert but Mom had to work.

5. Our teacher is nice and she loves dogs.

6. Sara will play the piano or she will sing.

7. I asked Lee to play ball but he was busy.

ELPS 5F

B **Write compound sentences using the pairs of sentences below. Use the connecting word in parentheses to complete each sentence. Remember to add commas!**

Do you see the bees? Can you hear them? (or)
Do you see the bees, or can you hear them?

1. Bees are busy. They all have jobs to do. *(and)*

_____

_____

_____

2. Most bees work. The queen bee does not work. *(but)*

_____

_____

_____

3. Bees care for the queen. They make honey. *(or)*

_____

_____

_____

Name _____

Commas to Set Off a Speaker's Words

When you write a speaker's exact words, you may tell who is speaking at the **beginning** of the sentence, or at the **end** of the sentence. Use a comma to set off the speaker's words, as shown below.

> Mr. Kent said, "Kari, you may begin your report."
>
> "My report is on birds," Kari said.

A Put commas where they are needed in these sentences.

"Many birds migrate in the winter," Kari said.

Darrin asked "What does *migrate* mean?"

"Migrate means that some birds go to a new place in winter" Kari answered. She added "Birds migrate to find food and water."

"That's very interesting" said Mr. Kent.

 **Write questions that Bill and Regina might ask about birds and migration. Use question marks and commas correctly.**

Bill asked ___ "_____

_____

_____ "

Regina asked ___ "_____

_____

_____ "

 **Write a question using a speaker's exact words. Include the speaker's name. Use quotation marks and a comma to set off the speaker's words.**

_____

_____

_____

ELPS 2C, 4C

Name _____

Comma Between a City and a State

Put a **comma** between the name of a city and a state.

Austin, Texas   Salem, Oregon

A Put commas between the cities and states below.

1. Calumet, Michigan   **4.** Portland Maine

2. Casper Wyoming   **5.** Dallas Texas

3. Williamsburg Virginia   **6.** Dayton Ohio

B Write the name of the city and state shown on page 460 in your *Write Source*. Then write the name of another city and its state. Put a comma between the city and state.

1. _____

2. _____

Draw a picture of a place in your city or town. Beneath your drawing, write sentences about your picture.

I live in _____

_____

_____

_____

_____

ELPS 2C, 4C

Name _____

Comma Between the Day and the Year

Put a **comma** between the day and the year.

January 17, 2011
November 12, 2011

October 2011

S	M	T	W	T	F	S
						1
2	3	4	5	6	7	8
9	10	(11)	12	13	14	15
16	17	18	19	20	21	22
23	◇24◇	25	26	27	28	29
30	31					

A Look at the calendar on this page. Then write the correct month, day, and year.

1. Write the date that is circled.

October 11, 2011

2. Write the date that has a diamond around it.

_____

3. Write the date for the last day of the month.

_____

4. Write the date for the first Wednesday of the month.

_____

B Write the dates for the following days. Be sure to include the month, day, and year. The months are listed on page 477 in *Write Source*.

1. Your next birthday:

_____

2. Today:

_____

3. Tomorrow:

_____

Write a true or make-believe sentence about the day you were born. Include the date of your birth in your sentence.

_____

_____

_____

_____

Name

Commas in Letters

Put **commas** after the greeting or salutation and the closing of a letter.

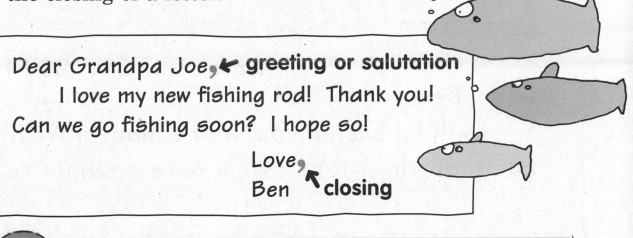

Dear Grandpa Joe,◄ **greeting or salutation**
   I love my new fishing rod! Thank you!
Can we go fishing soon? I hope so!
           Love,
          Ben ◄ **closing**

A   **Put commas where they belong in these letters.**

May 10, 2011

Dear Ben

   Ask your mom when your family is coming to Florida. Then we can go fishing.

     Love

     Grandpa Joe

May 18, 2011

Dear Grandpa Joe

   We are coming to see you on December 23rd. I can't wait! My tackle box is ready.

     Love

     Ben

26

Put commas in Grandpa's letter. Then pretend you are Ben. Write what you would say in your next letter to Grandpa Joe. Be sure to put commas in the right places.

November 24, 2011

Dear Ben

   I will be seeing you in one month! We'll camp out in a tent. We'll have a campfire.

         Love

         Grandpa Joe

_____

(Date)

_____

(Greeting or Salutation)

_____

_____

_____

(Closing)

_____

(Signature)

Name _____

Comma Review

This activity reviews comma uses you have learned.

 Put a comma between the names of the cities and the states in these sentences.

1. You can see mountains from Portland Oregon.

2. The James River goes through Richmond Virginia.

3. El Paso Texas, is near Mexico.

4. Sitka Alaska, is on the Pacific Ocean.

5. Hilo Hawaii, is part of an island.

 Put a comma between the day and the year in these sentences.

1. George Washington was born February 22 1732.

2. The first nickel was made on May 16 1866.

3. On February 7 1867, Laura Ingalls Wilder was born.

4. The astronaut Sally Ride was born May 26 1951.

C **Put commas between words in a series in these sentences.**

1. Red orange yellow and green are rainbow colors.

2. My uncle aunt and cousin live in Michigan.

3. Jonathan likes snowboarding sledding and skiing.

4. My family has two cats one dog and a turtle.

5. I send letters notes and e-mail messages.

D **Put commas where they are needed.**

Maggie asked "What kind of seashell is that?"

"It's a heart cockle" Molly said. "If you put two together, they form a heart."

"Amazing!" Maggie added. "What's this one?"

"It's called a turkey wing" Molly answered.

"That's a perfect name! It looks just like one" said Maggie.

★ **TEKS** 2.22C(ii)
ELPS 2C, 4C, 5E

Name _____

Making Contractions 1

A **contraction** turns two words into one word. To make a contraction, put an **apostrophe** where one or more letters are left out.

Two Words	Contraction
does not	doesn't
we have	we've

A In the second column, cross out the letters that are left out of the contraction in the first column.

Contraction	Two Words
1. I'm	I am
2. she'll	she will
3. he's	he is
4. they're	they are
5. he'd	he would
6. hasn't	has not
7. we'll	we will
8. shouldn't	should not

TEKS 2.22C(ii)
ELPS 5E

B Make contractions from the words below. Remember to use an apostrophe each time!

1. do not _____

2. that is _____

3. cannot _____

4. I have _____

C On each blank below, write the contraction for the words in parentheses.

1. _____ going to make a mask.
(I am)

2. _____ make it out of a paper bag.
(I will)

3. _____ going to be a scary mask.
(It is)

4. Dad _____ know I am making it.
(does not)

 2.22C(ii)
ELPS 2C, 4C, 5E

Name _____

Making Contractions 2

A **contraction** turns two words into one word. To make a contraction, put an **apostrophe** where one or more letters are left out.

Two Words	Contraction
she will	she'll

 A   In each sentence, underline the contraction. Then write the word or words the contraction stands for.

1. "Peter <u>didn't</u> obey Mom," said Flopsy. _did not_

2. "You can't go to the ball," she told Cinderella.

_____

3. "You wouldn't help me," said the Little Red Hen.

_____

4. "I couldn't sleep in that bumpy bed," said the princess.

_____

5. The wolf said, "I'll blow your house down." _____

6. "I'm a real boy!" shouted Pinocchio. _____

TEKS 2.22C(ii)
ELPS 5E

 **B** **Write the two words that each contraction stands for.**

1. doesn't _____

2. hasn't _____

3. he's _____

4. I've _____

5. isn't _____

6. it's _____

7. we're _____

8. you'll _____

 **Write a sentence using one of the contractions above.**

_____

_____

_____

TEKS 2.22C(iii)
ELPS 2C, 4C, 5E

Name

Apostrophes to Show Ownership 1

Add an **apostrophe** and an *s* to a word to show ownership.

Tom has a boat.   It is Tom's boat.

A   Each phrase below shows ownership. Draw a picture in each box.

the cat's rug	the bird's nest
Susan's jump rope	my mother's hat

34

 **B** Write the words below to show ownership. Be sure to add an apostrophe and an *s* to each word.

1. the _____ leaves
(tree)

2. the _____ string
(kite)

3. the _____ wing
(airplane)

4. the _____ tail
(bird)

C Write the names below to show ownership. Add an apostrophe and an *s* to each name.

1. I see _____ purple pencil.
(Maria)

2. This is _____ math book.
(Don)

3. _____ backpack is heavier than mine.
(Jane)

4. _____ idea notebook is on the desk.
(Sol)

2.22C(iii)
ELPS 5E

Name _____

Apostrophes to Show Ownership 2

Add an **apostrophe** and an **s** to a word to show ownership.

The cat's tail is white.

The cat's whiskers are white, too.

A **Add an apostrophe in each sentence to show ownership.**

1. Mollys cat is named Ink because he has black fur.

2. Roberts new kitten is as white as snow.

3. His cats name is Marshmallow.

4. Marshmallows fur looks brown after she plays in the garden.

5. Jennifers brown cat is named Cocoa.

6. Cocoas fur always stays brown, wherever she plays.

 **TEKS** 2.22C(iii)
ELPS 5E

B Put apostrophes where needed to show ownership in this letter.

November 11, 2010

Dear Uncle Frank,

I can hardly wait for Fathers Day. Dads friend Fernando is coming over. Fernandos stories about growing up in Brazil are amazing. Plus, he likes Nickys funny stories. Moms one wish is that her brother Frank could come!

Love,

Sam

 Now answer this question about the letter.

1. How many apostrophes did you add? _____

ELPS 2C, 4C

Name _____

Underlining Titles

Underline the titles of books and magazines.

a book — <u>Onion Sundaes</u>

a magazine — <u>3, 2, 1 Contact</u>

A **Underline the titles in the following sentences.**

1. My sister's favorite book is <u>Pocahontas</u>.

2. My grandmother has a book called Mrs. Bird.

3. Kids Discover is a magazine for kids.

4. The title of our book is Write Source.

5. Ranger Rick is a nature magazine for kids.

6. I just read Ira Sleeps Over by Bernard Waber.

7. My dad reads National Geographic every month.

8. Our teacher is reading All About Sam to us.

B Complete the following sentences. Remember to underline the titles.

1. My favorite book is _____

_____ .

2. My favorite magazine is _____

_____ .

3. The title of the last book I read is _____

_____ .

Draw a cover for one of your favorite books. Write the book title on your cover.

Name _____

Quotation Marks Before and After a Speaker's Words

Comic strips make it easy to tell who is speaking. They use speech balloons. Here Mom and Steve are talking about dinner.

When you write sentences, you use **quotation marks** to show the speaker's exact words.

Steve asked, "Mom, may we make pizza for dinner?"

"That sounds really good to me," Mom said.

40

 **Read the speech balloons. Then write the sentences below. Put quotation marks where they are needed.**

May we make pepperoni pizza?

Yes, Let's add something else.

Steve asked,_____

_____

Mom answered,_____

_____

How about mushrooms?

Great choice!

Steve asked,_____

_____

Mom said,_____

_____

Name _____

Punctuation Review

This review covers punctuation marks you have learned.

A   **Fill in each list below.**

Cat Names	City Names	Food Names
1. _Buddy_	1. _____	1. _____
2. _____	2. _____	2. _____
3. _____	3. _____	3. _____

B   **Use your lists to write sentences.**

1. Write a **telling sentence** about three cats.

_____

_____

2. Write an **asking sentence** about three cities.

_____

_____

ELPS 5E

3. Write an **exciting sentence** about three foods.

_____

_____

C Write contractions for the words below.

1. did not _____   **6.** cannot _____

2. you are _____   **7.** we have _____

3. I am _____   **8.** has not _____

4. it is _____   **9.** is not _____

5. they will _____   **10.** she is _____

D Fill in each blank with a word that shows ownership.

1. The dog has a ball. It is the _____ ball.

2. Alisha has a computer. It is _____ computer.

3. Our teacher has a bike. It is our _____ bike.

4. Barry has a pet bird. It is _____ pet bird.

Name _____

Capital Letters for Names and Titles

Use **capital letters** for people's names and titles.

title   **name**

Mr. Thomas lives in a little house.
Mrs. Thomas lives there, too.

Add capital letters where they are needed. Cross out the lower-case letter you want to change. Write the correct capital letter above it.

                M   C

1. Our class helper is m̷rs. c̷antu.

2. The school nurse is mr. thomas.

3. Yesterday, will and I went to see dr. paula.

4. I asked ms. demarko to read me a story.

5. Mr. and mrs. chang picked us up at camp.

6. Tomorrow, ms. banks and sally are coming over.

7. Our dentist is dr. villa.

 **Draw a picture or paste a photo of your favorite grown-up.**

 **Write two sentences telling why you like this grown-up. Make sure to use the grown-up's title and name each time.**

1. _____

_____

2. _____

_____

Name _____

Capital Letters for Days of the Week 1

Use **capital letters** for days of the week.

Sunday   **W**ednesday

A Answer the questions below. Remember to use capital letters correctly.

1. Which day comes after Saturday? _____Sunday_____

2. Which day is between Tuesday and Thursday?

_____

3. Which day begins with the letter "F"? _____

4. Which day is the first day of the school week?

_____

5. Which day comes after Friday? _____

6. Which day is before Wednesday? _____

7. Which day comes before Friday? _____

 TEKS 2.22B(ii)

 **Put the days of the week in the correct order, starting with Sunday.**

Thursday   Sunday   Tuesday   Monday

Friday   Wednesday   Saturday

1. _____

2. _____

3. _____

4. _____

5. _____

6. _____

7. _____

Write a sentence about your favorite day of the week.

_____

_____

_____

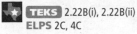

TEKS 2.22B(i), 2.22B(ii)
ELPS 2C, 4C

Name _____

Capital Letters for Days of the Week 2

Use **capital letters** for days of the week.

↗Saturday
↗Thursday

 A **Write each day of the week with a capital letter.**

1. Mr. Shaw will be here tuesday, March 13.

Tuesday _____

2. The party was on friday, September 23.

_____

3. School starts monday, August 16.

_____

4. Kathleen's birthday is wednesday, April 29.

_____

5. Valentine's Day will be thursday, February 14.

_____

★ TEKS 2.22B(ii)

 Put a capital letter at the beginning of each day of the week.

Everyone in my family was born on a different day of the week. Mom was born on a tuesday, but dad was born on a friday. My sister Lisa was born on a thursday night, and I was born early one saturday morning. Then my brand new dog Biscuit was born last sunday!

 **Write two sentences about activities you have on certain days.**

1. _____

   _____

2. _____

   _____

TEKS 2.22B(i), 2.22B(ii)
ELPS 2C, 4C

Name _____

Capital Letters for Months of the Year 1

Use **capital letters** for the months of the year.

February   May

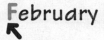

 A **Use capital letters for the months in these sentences.**

                                              M

1. The first day of spring is in march.

2. The first day of summer is in june.

3. The first day of fall is in september.

4. The first day of winter is in december.

5. The first month of the year is january.

6. The shortest month is february.

7. Usually july and august are the hottest months.

8. april showers bring spring flowers.

50

★ TEKS 2.22B(ii)

B Here are three more months. Write each month correctly.

may _____

october _____

november _____

Write one sentence about each month above.

1. _____

_____

_____

2. _____

_____

_____

3. _____

_____

Name _____

Capital Letters for Months of the Year 2

Use **capital letters** for the months of the year.

A Read the sentences below. Write the month correctly on the line after each sentence.

1. Handwriting Day is the 12th of january. ___January___

2. Groundhog Day is in february. _____

3. Arbor Day is in april. _____

4. Memorial Day is the last Monday in may. _____

5. My birthday is in june. _____

6. Independence Day is the fourth of july. _____

7. Labor Day is in september. _____

8. Fire Prevention Week is during october. _____

9. Thanksgiving Day is in november. _____

TEKS 2.22B(ii)

 **Unscramble these months and write them correctly on the lines below. Remember to use a capital letter for the first letter!**

1. uejn   *June* _____

2. gsatuu   _____

3. hamrc   _____

4. yrjnuaa   _____

5. larip   _____

6. yma   _____

7. tbreoco   _____

8. eeedmbcr   _____

9. eyfbarru   _____

10. ljuy   _____

11. ervbnome   _____

12. tpbreesme   _____

TEKS 2.22B(i)
ELPS 2C, 4C

53

Name _____

Capital Letters for Holidays

Use **capital letters** for the names of holidays.

↖   ↖
Father's Day   Thanksgiving Day

A Use capital letters for the holidays in these sentences. (*Day* is part of many holiday names.)

N Y D
1. new year's day is in January.

2. We made cards for valentine's day.

3. We celebrate presidents' day in February.

4. mother's day and memorial day are always in May.

5. One holiday in June is flag day.

6. July 4 is independence day.

7. The first Monday in September is labor day.

8. The second Monday in October is columbus day.

TEKS 2.22B(i)

B Write the names of three holidays found in the sentences on page 51.

1. _____

2. _____

3. _____

Now use the names of those three holidays in sentences.

1. _____

_____

_____

2. _____

_____

_____

3. _____

_____

_____

 **TEKS** 2.22B(i)
ELPS 2C, 4C

Name _____

Capital Letters
for Names of Places

Use a **capital letter** for the name
of a city, a state, or a country.

City   **State**   **Country**

Carson City   Nevada   France
Rome   Iowa   Mexico

 A   **Write the city, state, or country correctly in the
following sentences.**

1. *Make Way for Ducklings* takes place in the city of

boston. _____**Boston**_____

2. The Everglades are in florida. _____

3. My grandma is from ireland. _____

4. Mt. Fuji is in japan. _____

5. The Willis Tower is in chicago. _____

6. The Peach State is georgia. _____

7. The capital of Alaska is juneau. _____

 TEKS 2.22B(i)

 **Write the answers to the following questions. Use correct capitalization.**

1. Which city or town do you live in?

_____

2. Which state do you live in?

_____

3. What is one state that is near your home state?

_____

4. What city does the President of the United States

live in?

_____

5. What country were you born in?

_____

6. Which country would you most like to visit?

_____

Name
_____

Capital Letter for *I*

Use a **capital letter** for the word *I*.

↗ I have curly red hair.

Cory and I like to tap-dance.

 Write the word *I* in each of these sentences.

1. Jimmy and ___I___ are friends.

2. Sometimes _____ go to his house.

3. _____ ride there on my bike.

4. Sometimes Jimmy and _____ play at the park.

 Write two sentences of your own using the word *I*.

1. _____

_____

2. _____

_____

Draw a picture of yourself in the box below. Then write three sentences about yourself. Use the word / in each sentence.

1. _____

_____

2. _____

_____

3. _____

_____

ELPS 2C, 4C

Name _____

Capital Letters to Begin Sentences

Always use a **capital letter** for the first word in a sentence.

We go to the park in the summer.

A Begin each of the following sentences with a capital letter.

1. One
   øne day we had a picnic.

2. aunt Jill brought a big bowl of fruit salad.

3. grandma made lemonade and biscuits.

4. we had sub sandwiches and carrot sticks.

5. all the kids played softball before lunch.

6. after the game everyone drank lemonade.

7. grandma's biscuits were the best part of the picnic.

8. the ants liked the crumbs we dropped.

B Put a capital letter at the beginning of each sentence. Put a period at the end of each sentence.

there's a swimming pool at our park sometimes we go there for a swim i learned how to swim last year now I can go in the deep end of the pool my little sister can't swim yet she stays in the shallow end maybe I'll teach her how to swim

Write two sentences about things you like to do in the summer. Remember to use capital letters and periods.

1. _____

_____

2. _____

_____

3. _____

_____

ELPS 2C, 4C

61

Name _____

Capital Letter for a Speaker's First Word

Use a **capital letter** for a speaker's first word.

He asked, "Can you guess what this is?"

A   Add capital letters where they are needed.

1. Our teacher asked, "do you know the story of the blind

   men and the elephant?"

2. "i do," said Jasmine. "one man feels the elephant's

   trunk. he thinks an elephant is like a big snake."

3. "another man feels the ear," Kerry added. "he thinks

   an elephant is like a big fan."

4. Jasmine said, "another man feels the leg. he thinks an

   elephant is like a tree trunk."

5. Then Ms. Tyler asked, "how could they know the truth?"

6. Kerry said, "they could work and talk together."

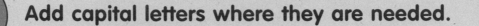

B **Add capital letters where they are needed.**

1. Ms. Tyler said, "that's right, Kerry."

2. She asked, "when do you like to work together?"

3. Kerry answered, "i like working together to perform plays."

4. Jasmine added, "that's something one person can't usually do alone."

Complete this sentence telling what the elephant thinks about the blind men.

The elephant said, "_____

_____."

ELPS 2C, 4C

Name _____

Capital Letters for Book Titles

Most words in book titles begin with **capital letters.**

➤ Town Mouse, Country Mouse

Some words do not begin with capital letters (unless they are the first or last word of a title). Here are some examples:

a an the and but of

to with by for on

 A **Write the four underlined book titles correctly on the lines below.**

I went to the library yesterday. I found some wonderful books! I checked out <u>madison in new york</u>, <u>fishing with dad</u>, <u>hattie and the fox</u>, and <u>my brother needs a boa</u>.

1. <u>Madison in New York</u>

2. _____

3. _____

4. _____

B **Write down the titles of your favorite book and magazine.**

Book: _____

Magazine: _____

Write a note telling someone about your favorite book or magazine.

Dear_____,

_____

_____

_____

_____

_____

Your friend,

_____

Name _____

Capital Letters for Greetings and Closings in Letters

Use a **capital letter** to begin the greeting and the closing in a letter.

Dear Grandpa,   **greeting or salutation**

Thank you for the new jacket. It's my favorite color! You always know just what I like.

Love,
Sara   **closing**

A Use capital letters to begin the greeting and closing in these letters.

July 1, 2010

dear Jake,
    Happy birthday! I wish I could go to your party. Will you have a piñata?
        love,
        Erin

May 21, 2011

dear Mr. Murphy,
    Your dog Sonny is one of the best dogs. May I walk him after school? I even have my own leash.
        thank you,
        Justin

TEKS 2.22B(iii)

 **B** Use capital letters to begin the greeting and closing in Aunt Molly's letter. Then pretend you are Harrison. Write what you would say back. Be sure to use capital letters in the right places.

July 14, 2010

dear Harrison,

    I hope you can come to Texas sometime soon. You have got to see the San Antonio River Walk! It's a great place to visit!

        love,

        Aunt Molly

_____

(Date)

_____

(Greeting or Salutation)

_____

_____

_____

(Closing)

_____

(Signature)

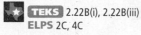
Name _____

Capital Letters Review

This activity reviews some of the different ways to use **capital letters**.

A **Put capital letters where they are needed. (There are 21 in all.) Watch for these things:**
* ✳ **salutations and closings,**
* ✳ **first word in a sentence,**
* ✳ **names and titles of people, and**
* ✳ **names of cities, states, and countries.**

May 24, 2010

dear linny,

our class is studying rivers. mr. banks read a

book to us about the nashua river. the book was

written by lynne cherry. we also learned about the

nile river in africa. ms. johnson visited our class. she

went down the amazon river on a raft!

love,

jim

TEKS 2.22B(i), 2.22B(ii)

B Put capital letters where they are needed. (There are 11 in all.) Watch for:
* a speaker's first word.
* names of days and months.
* names of holidays.

1. Joel said, "my favorite day is sunday. What's yours?"

2. "sunday is my favorite day, too," I answered.

3. "what's your favorite month?" Molly asked.

4. I said, "my favorite month is july, because it's summer, and that's when I was born."

5. Molly said, "my favorite month is december, because that's when we celebrate hanukkah."

6. "that's when we celebrate christmas," I said.

C Put capital letters where they are needed in these titles.

1. the tigger movie

2. the fox and the hound

Name _____

Plurals

Plural means more than one. For most nouns, make the plurals by adding **-s**.

desk → desk**s** window → window**s**

 Here is a list of things that may be in your classroom. Write the plural forms of the nouns. Then tell a partner a sentence using the plural form of something else found in your classroom.

1. flag _____ flags _____

2. table _____

3. eraser _____

4. pencil _____

5. book _____

6. marker _____

7. door _____

8. ruler _____

TEKS 2.21A(ii)
ELPS 2C, 2G, 2H, 2I, 3E, 4C

 **B** **Fill in the blanks by changing the singular word under the line into a plural word.**

There are 16 _____ and 10 _____
   (girl)   (boy)

in my class this year. We have one teacher and two

_____ . There are three learning
   (helper)

_____ in the classroom. In the reading center
   (center)

there are lots of _____ . The art center has
                     (magazine)

some very bright _____ . In the writing center
                    (marker)

there's a whole box of _____ and many different
                          (pencil)

_____ of paper. I love my classroom!
   (kind)

Write a sentence telling how many boys and girls there are in your class. Then tell a partner how many students are in your class using a complete sentence.

_____

_____

TEKS 2.21A(ii)
ELPS 2C, 2G, 2H, 2I, 3E, 4C

Name _____

Plurals Using
-s and -es 1

For most nouns, make the **plurals** by adding **-s**.

one bird   two birds
a bike   four bikes

For some nouns, you need to do more.
Add **-es** to words that end in **sh, ch, s,** or **x**.

a bush   some bushes
one box   two boxes

A   Write the plurals of the following nouns. It's easy—just add **-s**. Then tell a sentence to a partner using one of the plural nouns.

1. bug   bugs
2. river _____
3. eye _____
4. ear _____
5. sister _____
6. dog _____
7. house _____
8. desk _____
9. tree _____
10. lake _____

72

TEKS 2.21A(ii)
ELPS 2C, 2G, 2H, 2I, 3E, 4C

B Make the following nouns plural. They all end in *sh*, *ch*, *s*, or *x*. You will need to add *-es*.

1. brush _____   **5.** fax _____

2. class _____   **6.** patch _____

3. bench _____   **7.** boss _____

C Fill in each blank with the correct plural. You will need to add *-s* to some nouns and *-es* to other nouns. Then use one of the plural nouns in your own sentence and tell it to a partner.

1. At the petting zoo there are baby _____
  (lion)

  and _____ .
    (fox)

2. There are three _____ and
      (hamster)

  two _____ in my classroom.
    (gerbil)

3. My mom makes _____ for me and
        (lunch)

  my two _____ .
    (brother)

Name _____

Plurals Using
-*s* and -*es* 2

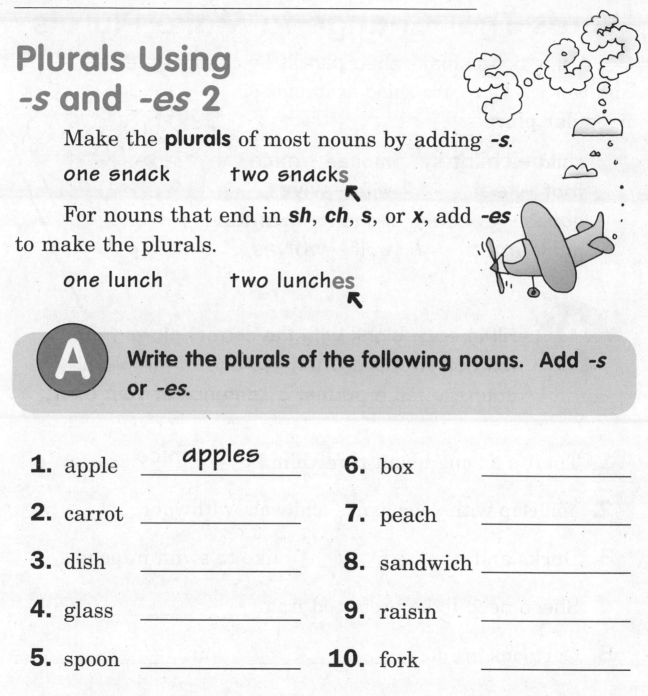

Make the **plurals** of most nouns by adding -*s*.

one snack   two snacks

For nouns that end in **sh**, **ch**, **s**, or **x**, add -*es* to make the plurals.

one lunch   two lunches

A   **Write the plurals of the following nouns. Add -*s* or -*es*.**

1. apple   _apples_

2. carrot   _____

3. dish   _____

4. glass   _____

5. spoon   _____

6. box   _____

7. peach   _____

8. sandwich _____

9. raisin   _____

10. fork   _____

KEEP GOING

Draw a lunchbox on your own paper. Include some of the things you just listed. Tell a partner about your lunch.

⭐ **TEKS** 2.21A(ii)
ELPS 2C, 2G, 2H, 2I, 3E, 4C

Words That Change to Make Plurals

A few nouns make their **plurals** by changing letters and words. Here are some examples of irregular plurals.

child – **children** ✎   mouse – **mice**
foot – **feet**   wife – **wives**
goose – **geese**   woman – **women**
man – **men**   wolf – **wolves**

A   Fill in each blank with the correct plural from the nouns above. Then use one of the plural nouns to tell a partner a sentence of your own.

1. There's a song about three blind _____ *mice* _____ .

2. You clap with your hands and walk with your _____ .

3. Ducks and _____ like to swim in ponds.

4. Sheep need to be protected from _____ .

5. Cartoons are for _____, but_____

and _____ watch them, too.

6. Husbands have _____ .

TEKS 2.21A(ii)
ELPS 2C, 2G, 2H, 2I, 3E, 4C

Name _____

Plurals of Words That End in *y* 1

Here are two rules for making **plurals** of nouns ending in *y*.

Rule 1 If there is a consonant right before the *y*, change the *y* to *i* and add **-es**.

one ba**b**y   two bab**ies**

Rule 2 If there is a vowel right before the *y*, just add **-s**.

one turk**e**y ➡ three turkey**s**

A Write the plurals of the following nouns. Use rule 1. Then tell a partner a sentence using one of the plural nouns.

1. cherry _____

2. kitty _____

3. party _____

4. berry _____

5. guppy _____

6. bunny _____

7. pony _____

8. puppy _____

9. country _____

10. worry _____

TEKS 2.21A(ii)
ELPS 2C, 2G, 2H, 2I, 3E, 4C

B Make the following nouns plural. Use rule 2 from page 75. Tell a partner a sentence using one of the plural nouns.

1. monkey _____

3. toy _____

2. ray _____

4. holiday _____

Circle three of the plurals you made on pages 75–76. Use each one in a sentence.

1. _____

_____

2. _____

_____

3. _____

_____

TEKS 2.21A(ii)
ELPS 2C, 2G, 2H, 2I, 3E, 4C

Name _____

Plurals of Words That End in *y* 2

Here are two rules for making **plurals** of nouns ending in *y*.

Rule 1   If there is a consonant right before the *y*, change the *y* to *i* and add *-es*.

one bab**y**   two bab**ies**

Rule 2   If there is a vowel right before the *y*, just add *-s*.

one turk**ey**   three turk**eys**

A   **Make the following nouns plural using rule 1 or rule 2. Then tell a partner a sentence using one of the plural nouns.**

1. story   _____stories_____

2. diary   _____

3. donkey   _____

4. key   _____

5. baby   _____

6. day   _____

TEKS 2.21A(ii)
ELPS 2C, 2G, 2H, 2I, 3E, 4C

Plurals Review

This activity reviews making **plurals**. After each set, practice speaking using plural nouns with a partner.

A Make these nouns plural by adding *-s* or *-es*.

1. glass _____

2. brush _____

3. frog _____

4. bus _____

5. dress _____

6. worm _____

B Make these nouns plural by adding *-s* or changing *y* to *i* and adding *-es*.

1. monkey _____

2. puppy _____

3. day _____

4. turkey _____

5. toy _____

6. cherry _____

C Change these words to make them plural.

1. mouse _____

2. foot _____

3. woman _____

4. knife _____

★ ELPS 2C, 4C

Name _____

Abbreviations

Put a **period** after a person's title.

Mr.   Mrs.   Ms.   Dr.

Ms. Walters   Mr. Johnson

A **Put periods after the people's titles in these sentences.**

1. Mr. Forest is our next-door neighbor.

2. Mr and Mrs Forest have a very big garden.

3. Mrs Forest works in her garden on cool mornings.

4. Her friend Dr Maynard stops to visit before work.

5. Mrs Forest gives Dr Maynard some pretty flowers to take to the office.

6. After dinner, Mr Forest likes to weed the garden.

7. Mrs Forest helps him water the plants.

B Think of four people who work in your school. Write their names below. Be sure to write Mr., Mrs., Ms., or Dr. before each.

1. _____

2. _____

3. _____

4. _____

Choose two of the people.
Write a sentence about each person.

1. _____

_____

2. _____

_____

Name _____

Abbreviations for Days and Months

When writing sentences, you should write the full names of the days and the months.

Today is **Tuesday**, **October** 9.

You should also know the **abbreviations** for the names of the days and the months.

Tuesday → **Tues.**   October → **Oct.**

A   Write the abbreviations for the days and months in the following lists.

1. Sunday   Sun. _____

2. Friday   _____

3. Wednesday   _____

4. Thursday   _____

5. Saturday   _____

6. Monday   _____

7. February   _____

8. March   _____

9. November   _____

10. August   _____

11. September   _____

12. January   _____

Post Office Abbreviations

The US Postal Service suggests using all capital letters and no periods in abbreviations.

948 **N** LINCOLN
North

A Read the addresses below. Write the words for the underlined abbreviations.

1. 1060 W ADDISON <u>ST</u>

Street

2. 1600 PENNSYLVANIA <u>AVE</u>

_____

3. 28 <u>E</u> 20TH ST

_____

4. 7400 GRANT <u>RD</u>

_____

5. 413 <u>S</u> EIGHTH STREET

_____

6. 40 PRESIDENTIAL <u>DR</u>

_____

Name _____

Checking Mechanics Review 1

This activity reviews some of the ways to use capital letters.

 A **Put capital letters where they are needed. There are 21 for you to find.**

dear theresa,

    how are you? how is life in florida? today ms.

martinez said she wished we could all visit you. i

told her i get to visit you in june!

    i just read a book called <u>lon po po</u>. it is a

good story from china. lee gave me the book for my

birthday.

    mrs. james said she hopes you like your new

school. do you?

                                        Your friend,

                                        Roger

B Fill in the blanks below. Use your *Write Source* if you need help.

1. Write two days of the week that are school days:

   _____   _____

2. Write the name of a holiday: _____

3. Write your first name: _____

4. Write the name of a planet: _____

5. Write your teacher's name: _____

Now use the words you just wrote to complete this story.

It was _____ , but there was no school. It
        (day of the week)

was _____ . _____ had a busy
    (name of the holiday)   *(teacher's name)*

day planned. _____ was going to build a
             (your name)

spaceship and blast off to _____ .
                           (planet)

ELPS 2C, 4C

Name _____

Checking Mechanics Review 2

This activity reviews plurals and abbreviations.

A Write the plural of each animal name.

1. cow _____   6. mouse _____

2. donkey _____   7. fox _____

3. finch _____   8. pig _____

4. goose _____   9. puppy _____

5. guppy _____   10. turkey _____

B Write the abbreviation for each day of the week.

1. Monday _____   5. Friday _____

2. Tuesday _____   6. Saturday _____

3. Wednesday _____   7. Sunday _____

4. Thursday _____

Write the abbreviations for the months of the year. Notice some months are not abbreviated.

1. January _____

2. February _____

3. March _____

4. April _____

5. May _____

6. June _____

7. July _____

8. August _____

9. September _____

10. October _____

11. November _____

12. December _____

ELPS 1C, 2C, 4C, 5B

Name _____

Using the Right Word 1

Some words sound alike, but they have different spellings. They also have different meanings. These words are **homophones**. Here are two examples:

My bare hands are cold.

I saw a bear at the zoo.

A **Fill in each blank with *bare* or *bear*.**

1. The panda ____bear____ lives in China.

2. Our teacher puts a rug on the _____ floor.

3. This morning I found a picture of a koala _____ .

4. Bees stung the boy's _____ legs.

5. The sun felt warm on my _____ arms.

B **Write a sentence using *bare* and *bear*.**

_____

_____

88

 **Fill in each blank with *ate* or *eight* or *ant* or *aunt*.**

Suzzie **ate** two carrots today.
Spiders have **eight** legs.

I watched an **ant** crawl up the wall.
My **aunt** lives across town.

1. Last year my _____ visited friends in California.

2. A carpenter _____ loves to eat wood.

3. I counted _____ sparrows sitting on the ground.

4. An _____ can walk on the ceiling.

5. I can pick up _____ rocks with one hand.

6. For lunch, I _____ a cheese sandwich.

7. Sarai's _____ _____ a tasty apple.

D **Write a sentence using *ate* and *eight*.**

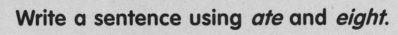

_____

_____

Name _____

Using the Right Word 2

Some words sound alike, but they have different spellings. They also have different meanings. These words are **homophones**. Here are two examples:

The **deer** eat acorns.   My aunt is **dear** to me.

A Fill in each blank with *blew* or *blue*.

The wind **blew** all day.
Some houses are painted **blue**.

1. Is _____blue_____ the color of the sky?

2. Please pick up a _____ worksheet today.

3. That girl just _____ a huge bubble.

4. Will you put this book on the _____ shelf?

5. The sign just _____ over.

B Write a sentence using *dear* and *deer*.

_____

_____

★ ELPS 1C, 5B, 5E

C Fill in each blank with *by* or *buy*.

Your pencil is **by** the dictionary.
I want to **buy** a notebook.

1. Can you _____ a bicycle for ten cents?

2. My best friend is waiting _____ the oak

tree in the park.

3. Will wants to _____ a birthday present

for Samuel.

4. The book _____ the teacher's desk

belongs to Maria.

5. Go stand _____ the school bus.

D Write a sentence using *for* and *four*.

_____

_____

ELPS 1C, 2C, 4C, 5B

Name _____

Using the Right Word 3

Some words sound alike, but they have different spellings. They also have different meanings. These words are **homophones**. Here are some examples:

I **hear** you.   I am **here**.

A   Fill in each blank with *here* or *hear*.

1. I asked my dog Dan to come _____here_____ .

2. Can you _____ what I am saying?

3. Did you _____ what happened to Sara?

4. _____ is the ball I thought I lost.

B   Fill in each blank with *no* or *know*.

Anna said, **"No**, I didn't **know** that."

1. There is _____ more soup.

2. I _____ where to get some.

3. Just answer yes or _____ .

4. Do you _____ the new girl?

ELPS 1C, 5B

 **Fill in each blank with *new* or *knew*.**

These shoes are **new**.   I **knew** the answer.

1. I got a _____ new _____ raincoat.

2. My mom _____ it was going to rain today.

3. Mike said he _____ how it would end.

4. My sister got _____ boots.

D **Fill in each blank with *its* or *it's*.**

It's washing **its** kitten.

1. The cat uses _____ tongue.

2. _____ washing the kitten's fur.

3. The kitten needs _____ mother.

4. _____ fun to watch the kitten grow.

E **Write a sentence using *its* and *it's*.**

_____

_____

Name _____

Using the Right Word 4

Some words sound alike, but they have different spellings. They also have different meanings. These words are **homophones**. Here are some examples:

I have two cats.
I have a dog, too.
I go to Pine Elementary.

A **Fill in each blank with *two*, *to*, or *too*.**
Too can mean "also" or "more than enough."

1. We are going _____to_____ the beach.

2. We can only stay for _____ hours.

3. Can Marla come, _____ ?

4. I like to take a radio _____ the beach.

5. Just don't play it _____ loud.

B **Write a sentence using *two* and *to*.**

_____

_____

 ELPS 1C, 5B, 5E

C Fill in each blank with *one* or *won*.

One summer I **won** a ribbon.

1. There was _____ race.

2. I was so fast, I _____.

3. Mr. Wang gave me _____ blue ribbon.

4. I showed it to _____ of my cousins.

5. My mom couldn't believe I _____.

D Fill in each blank with *their*, *there*, or *they're*.

We saw **their** new puppy. (*Their* shows ownership.)

There are three pets now.

They're lots of fun. (*They're* = they are.)

1. _____There_____ are four kids in the Clark family.

2. We play freeze tag in _____ backyard.

3. _____ my next-door neighbors.

4. I went to school _____ for one year.

ELPS 1C, 2C, 4C, 5B

Name _____

Using the Right Word
Review 1

This activity reviews the
homophones you have practiced.

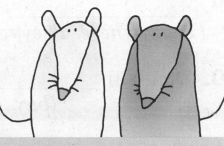

A   Write the correct word in each blank.

1. Sam took _____**two**_____ rats _____ school.
  (two, to, too)   *(two, to, too)*

2. The white rat _____ all of _____ food.
  (eight, ate)   *(its, it's)*

3. Someone yelled, "Don't bring them in _____ !"
  (hear, here)

4. "I don't like _____ _____ tails!"
  (they're, their, there)   *(bear, bare)*

5. Miss Green said, "I _____ what to do."
  (no, know)

6. "We'll get a box _____ the rats to sleep in."
  (for, four)

7. Other students have pets _____ .
  (two, to, too)

ELPS 1C, 5B

8. Don has a _____ pet parrot.
(new, knew)

9. _____ are more than 300 kinds of parrots.
(Their, There, They're)

10. Don will _____ a book about parrots.
(buy, by)

11. Then he will _____ how to care for his pet.
(no, know)

12. You should _____ the parrot talk!
(hear, here)

B   **Write three sentences. Use one of these words in each sentence: *to, two, too*.**

1. _____

_____

2. _____

_____

3. _____

_____

ELPS 1C, 5B, 5E

Name _____

Using the Right Word Review 2

A Before each sentence is a group of words.
Choose the correct word to fill in each blank.

1. **(hear, here)** "Did you _____ that Uncle Andy and

   Aunt Sue are coming _____ ?" I asked.

2. **(know, no)** "Well, _____ , I didn't _____

   that," Lea answered.

3. **(Ant, Aunt)** _____ Sue got a sailboat," I said. "She

   painted a red _____ on the side of the boat."

4. **(their, there, they're)** "I hope _____ bringing

   _____ boat when they come," Lea said.

5. **(knew, new)** "Sure," I said. "They _____ we'd

   want to sail in the _____ boat."

★ ELPS 1C, 5B

B **Below are three homophone pairs. Pick one pair, and draw a picture showing those words. (Use *Write Source* if you need to check meanings.) Then write a sentence about your picture.**

one won   blew blue   dear deer

_____

_____

_____

Sentence Activities

This section includes activities related to basic sentence writing, kinds of sentences, and sentence problems. In addition, **KEEP GOING**, which is at the end of many activities, encourages follow-up practice of certain skills.

ELPS 2C, 4C

Name _____

Understanding Sentences

A **sentence** tells a complete thought.

This is not a complete thought:
On the window.

This is a complete thought:
A bug is on the window.

A Check whether each group of words is a complete thought or not.

	Complete Thought	
	Yes	**No**
1. From the downstairs music room.	_____	✓
2. The sound was very loud.	_____	_____
3. Covered his ears.	_____	_____
4. After that.	_____	_____
5. He shut the front door.	_____	_____
6. Max played the drums.	_____	_____
7. Ming played the piano.	_____	_____
8. Mom the silver flute.	_____	_____

★ ELPS 4C

B Fill in each blank with a word that completes the thought.

1. _____ was playing with a ball.

2. The _____ rolled down the hill.

3. _____ ran after it.

4. Then a big, hairy _____ ran after it, too.

5. The _____ got the ball and kept running.

6. Was the _____ gone for good?

Draw a picture about sentence 4.

ELPS 2C, 4C

Name _____

Parts of a Sentence 1

Every **sentence** has two parts, the **subject** and the **predicate**. The subject is the naming part. The predicate tells what the subject is doing. It always includes the verb.

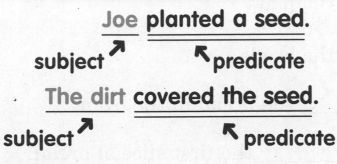

A Underline the subject with one line. Underline the predicate with two lines.

1. Joe watered his seed every day.

2. He watched it carefully.

3. A leaf popped out.

4. The leaf grew larger.

5. A flower bloomed one morning.

6. Joe told his mom.

ELPS 4C

B Write a verb for each sentence.

1. Mom _____ bread.

2. I _____ her.

3. I _____ the flour.

4. I _____ the bowls.

5. Mom _____ the bread in the oven.

6. I always _____ the first slice of bread.

C Check whether the underlined words are the subject or the predicate of the sentence.

	Subject	Predicate
1. Your body <u>has a lot of bones</u>.		✓
2. <u>Your longest bone</u> is in your leg.		
3. Your ribs <u>look like a cage</u>.		
4. Your smallest bone <u>is in your ear</u>.		
5. <u>Jellyfish</u> have no bones.		
6. <u>A skeleton</u> is all bones.		

Name

Parts of a Sentence 2

Every **sentence** has two parts, the **subject** and the **predicate**. The subject is the naming part. The predicate tells what the subject is doing. It always includes the verb.

Haley came to the party.

subject ↗   ↖predicate

A **Fill in each blank with a word from the box. You may use some words more than once. These words are the subjects in your sentences.**

Poems	**Ms. Day**	**Sam**	**Tacos**
Eddy	**Winter**	**Roses**	**Sarah**

1. _____ plays on the soccer team.

2. Last summer, _____ drove to Ohio.

3. _____ grow in Grandpa's garden.

4. _____ are my favorite food.

5. _____ sleeps in a tent.

106

 ELPS 4C

B Fill in each blank with a verb from the box. You will use each word only once. Each verb will be included in the predicate part of the sentence.

| learned | barked | is | went |
| hit | sang | eats | gave |

1. Bobby _____ a home run.

2. The dog _____ loudly.

3. Steve _____ toast every morning.

4. Our teacher _____ us a test.

5. Kerry _____ a song for the class.

6. At camp, Cheri _____ to ride a horse.

7. My sister's name _____ Gail.

8. We all _____ for a hike yesterday.

TEKS 2.21C
ELPS 2C, 2G, 2H, 2I, 3C, 3E, 4C

Name _____

Kinds of Sentences 1

A **telling sentence** makes a statement. Put a period after a telling sentence.
Buster is out in the rain.

An **asking sentence** asks a question. Put a question mark after an asking sentence.
Where is Buster?

A Write *T* before each telling sentence, and put a period after it. Write *A* before each asking sentence, and put a question mark after it. Then ask a partner a question and have him or her answer it with a telling sentence.

___A___ **1.** What is Sandy doing**?**

_____ **2.** Sandy is making a bird feeder

_____ **3.** Why is she doing that

_____ **4.** She wants to see what kinds of birds will come

_____ **5.** Where will she put the bird feeder

_____ **6.** She's going to hang it in a tree

_____ **7.** What kind of food will she put in it

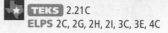 TEKS 2.21C
ELPS 2C, 2G, 2H, 2I, 3C, 3E, 4C

B Draw a picture of some birds at a bird feeder.

 Write one telling sentence and one asking sentence about your picture. Then have a partner ask you a question about your picture. Answer with a telling sentence.

1. Telling Sentence:_____

_____

2. Asking Sentence:_____

_____

TEKS 2.21C
ELPS 2C, 2G, 2H, 2I, 3C, 3E, 4C

Name _____

Kinds of Sentences 2

A **telling sentence** makes a statement. Put a period after a telling sentence.

I'll feed Buster.

An **asking sentence** asks a question. Put a question mark after an asking sentence.

Would you feed Buster, please?

A Write a telling sentence that is an answer for each asking sentence. Make sure you write complete sentences. Then ask a partner which question they liked answering best.

1. What happened to your shoes?

_____

2. Who left the door open?

_____

3. How did you get all muddy?

_____

4. Have you read Too Many Tamales?

_____

★ **TEKS** 2.21C
ELPS 2C, 2G, 2H, 2I, 3C, 3E, 4C

B Pretend that you are only four years old. Write some asking sentences that a four-year-old might ask. Two examples have been done for you.

1. _Where do bugs come from?_

2. _Why does it get dark at night?_

3. _____

4. _____

5. _____

Pick two questions from above. Write telling sentences to answer them. (Write interesting answers that are complete sentences!) Then pick another question and tell your answer to a partner.

1. _____

_____

2. _____

_____

TEKS 2.21B
ELPS 2C, 2G, 2H, 2I, 3E, 4C, 5E

Name _____

Subject-Verb Agreement in Sentences

Subjects and **verbs** must agree in number.
A **singular** subject must have a singular verb.

I am at school today.

↗   ↖
Subject   Verb

A **plural** subject must have a plural verb.

We are at school today.

↗   ↖
Subject   Verb

 A **Write the verb that goes with the subject of each sentence.**

1. Sometimes we _____ *have* _____ a fire drill at school.
(has, have)

2. Mrs. Miller _____ is our fire marshall.
(is, are)

3. She _____ an orange vest so we can see her.
(wear, wears)

4. We _____ in one straight line.
(walk, walks)

5. Everyone _____ happy that it isn't a real fire!
(feel, feels)

TEKS 2.21B
ELPS 2C, 2G, 2H, 2I, 3E, 4C, 5E

B Fill in each blank with *have* or *has*.

1. We _____ have _____ cousins living in the country.

2. Our cousins _____ a farm.

3. The farm _____ a house and barn.

4. The barn _____ cows and horses inside.

C Fill in each blank with *run* or *runs*.

1. All the horses _____ really fast.

2. Patty's horse _____ in the front.

3. The other horses _____ behind her horse.

4. My horse_____ on the side of the road!

D Describe your home to a partner using the verbs *is* and *are*. Use correct subject-verb agreement.

ELPS 4C

Name _____

Sentence Review

This reviews what you have learned about sentences.

A Write *S* after each sentence. Write *X* after each group of words that is not a sentence.

1. My dad and I. _____

2. Went to Blue Hills Park. _____

3. We hiked to the top of a big hill. _____

4. Above the clouds! _____

5. Then Treasure Cave. _____

6. It was scary and dark inside. _____

7. Later, we saw three fat raccoons. _____

8. We had a lot of fun. _____

9. Will visit the park again. _____

B Read page 414 in your *Write Source* to see how the writer made one group of words a complete thought.

C Underline and label the subjects and the predicates in the sentences that begin with *I*. The first sentence has been done for you.

May 26, 2011

Dear Grandma,

             S   P

Guess what? <u>I</u> <u>lost another tooth</u>! I bit into an apple.

I feel the new hole in my mouth now.

    Mom will bring me to your house next week. I like your yard. I think your new slide is great!

    Will you make smoothies for me? See you soon.

            Love,

            John

Copy one telling sentence from the letter. Discuss with a partner if the sentence has correct subject-verb agreement.

1. Telling Sentence: _____

_____

Language Activities

The activities in this section are related to the parts of speech. All of the activities have a page link to the Student Edition of *Texas Write Source*. In addition, **KEEP GOING**, which is at the end of many activities, encourages follow-up practice of certain skills.

Name

_____

Nouns

A **noun** names a person, a place, or a thing.

Person	Place	Thing
student	park	pizza
friend	mall	candle

A Write what each noun is: *person*, *place*, or *thing*. Add three nouns of your own.

1. firefighter _____person_____

2. library _____

3. hammer _____

4. teacher _____

5. pencil _____

6. store _____

7. _____

8. _____

9. _____

ELPS 4C

B Write *N* if the word is a noun. Write *X* if the word is not a noun.

____ **1.** paper   ____ **4.** bring   ____ **7.** and

____ **2.** go   ____ **5.** girl   ____ **8.** hot

____ **3.** bee   ____ **6.** store   ____ **9.** kite

C Underline the noun in each sentence.

1. The bus is yellow.   **4.** Look at the duck!

2. The spider jumped.   **5.** The sky looks pretty.

3. This game is hard.   **6.** A friend called.

Write a sentence about your favorite toys. Then underline the nouns in your sentence.

_____

_____

_____

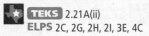

TEKS 2.21A(ii)
ELPS 2C, 2G, 2H, 2I, 3E, 4C

Name _____

Common and Proper Nouns 1

A **common noun** names a person, place, or thing.
A **proper noun** names a special person, place, or thing.

Common Noun	Proper Noun
boy	Tony Prada
school	Hill Elementary
city	Lexington

A proper noun begins with a capital letter.
Some proper nouns are more than one word.

A Underline the common noun in each sentence. Then tell a partner a sentence with a common noun and a proper noun. Have your partner identify each kind of noun.

1. The class is busy writing.

2. Our teacher likes to help.

3. A girl is reading quietly.

4. The street is shiny and wet.

5. This sandy beach is hot.

6. Let's swim in the pool!

★ **TEKS** 2.21A(ii)
ELPS 2C, 2G, 2H, 2I, 3E, 4C

B Underline the proper noun in each sentence.

1. We stopped at Jefferson Library.

2. Susie wanted a book about horses.

3. This book is about President Lincoln.

4. Principal Brown visited the library.

5. He speaks Spanish.

6. Rosa Perez does, too.

C Write *C* if the underlined word is a common noun. Write *P* if the underlined word is a proper noun. Then tell a partner your own sentences using common and proper nouns.

____ **1.** My neighbor walks her <u>dog</u> each afternoon.

____ **2.** My neighbor's name is <u>Mrs. Lee</u>.

____ **3.** Her dog likes <u>treats</u>.

____ **4.** <u>Alf</u> is a funny dog.

____ **5.** One day he got on a <u>bus</u>.

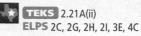
TEKS 2.21A(ii)
ELPS 2C, 2G, 2H, 2I, 3E, 4C

121

Name _____

Common and Proper Nouns 2

A **common noun** names any person, place, or thing. A **proper noun** names a special person, place, or thing.

Common Noun	Proper Noun
holiday	New Year's Day
country	Mexico

A proper noun begins with a capital letter. Some proper nouns are more than one word.

A Write **C** if the word is a common noun. Write **P** if the word is a proper noun. Choose two nouns from below to say in a sentence.

_C_ **1.** cat

_____ **2.** Sun Park

_____ **3.** library

_____ **4.** Washington, D.C.

_____ **5.** flag

_____ **6.** Jennifer

_____ **7.** Main Street

_____ **8.** book

_____ **9.** mountain

_____ **10.** Rocky Mountains

TEKS 2.21A(ii)
ELPS 2C, 2G, 2H, 2I, 3E, 4C

B Draw a line from each common noun to the proper noun that fits with it.

1. girl   United States

2. boy   Fluffy

3. cat   "The Three Bears"

4. country   Tom

5. story   Lisa

C Write *C* if the underlined noun is a common noun. Write *P* if the underlined noun is a proper noun. Choose your favorite noun from below. Use it in a sentence that you tell to a partner.

_____ 1. Today is <u>Christmas</u>!

_____ 2. There is no <u>school</u> today.

_____ 3. The <u>air</u> is freezing cold.

_____ 4. <u>Aunt Lizzie</u> visited us.

_____ 5. Kevin brought <u>popcorn</u>.

_____ 6. Chin is from <u>Korea</u>.

⭐ **TEKS** 2.21A(ii)
ELPS 2C, 2G, 2H, 2I, 3E, 4C

Name _____

Singular and Plural Nouns

Singular means one.

elephant

Plural means more than one.

elephant**s** ↙

Plural nouns usually end with **s**.

A Write **S** if the noun is singular. Write **P** if the noun is plural. Tell a partner a sentence using a plural noun and a singular noun from below.

__P__ **1.** boxes   ____ **4.** rug

____ **2.** table   ____ **5.** truck

____ **3.** chairs   ____ **6.** toys

B Write **S** if the underlined noun is singular. Write **P** if the underlined noun is plural.

____ **1.** I like <u>art</u>.   ____ **3.** <u>Paints</u> are messy.

____ **2.** I have <u>crayons</u>.   ____ **4.** It's for my <u>sister</u>.

★ TEKS 2.21A(ii)
ELPS 2C, 2G, 2H, 2I, 3E, 4C

C   Underline the plural noun in each sentence.

1. The cow has black and white spots.

2. Some piglets are pink.

3. Potatoes spilled out of the grocery bag.

4. My sister baked dinner rolls yesterday.

5. Tony took off his muddy shoes.

6. Erin held the tiny kittens.

Draw a picture about one of the plural nouns you underlined. Write the noun under your picture. Discuss your picture with a partner.

TEKS 2.22C(iii)
ELPS 2C, 4C, 5E

Name _____

Possessive Nouns

A **possessive noun** shows ownership.
A possessive noun has an **apostrophe**.

Tia's toy boat was left out in the yard.
(The toy boat belongs to Tia.)

After the storm, we found it in the **dog's** house.
(The house belongs to the dog.)

A Circle the possessive nouns.

1. (Mike's) story about Mr. Bug was fun to read.

2. Mr. Bug's house was flooded when it rained.

3. Mr. Bug's family hopped in a toy boat.

4. All the little Bugs waited for the storm's end.

5. Finally, the boat floated to a dog's house.

6. The dog's name was Buddy.

7. The little Bugs asked if they could share their new

   friend's home.

8. The story's title is "The Bugs Find a Buddy."

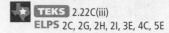 **TEKS** 2.22C(iii)
ELPS 2C, 2G, 2H, 2I, 3E, 4C, 5E

 Draw a picture of one of these things from the story:

 ✳ **Mr. Bug's flooded house.**
 ✳ **the child's toy boat.**
 ✳ **the dog's house.**

Talk with a partner about your picture. Use a possessive noun.

Name _____

Pronouns 1

A **pronoun** is a word that takes the place of a noun.

Noun	**Pronoun**
Todd did it.	He did it.
Sally laughed.	She laughed.
The rope broke.	It broke.
The skates are too big.	They are too big.

A Circle the pronouns that replace the underlined nouns in the sentences below. Then say a sentence using each of the pronouns below.

1. <u>Holly</u> gave Katy a Mexican coin.

(She) gave Katy a Mexican coin.

2. Katy put the <u>coin</u> in a safe place.

Katy put it in a safe place.

3. <u>Peggy and Jo</u> wanted to see the coin.

They wanted to see the coin.

4. Then <u>Jay</u> asked to see it, too.

Then he asked to see it, too.

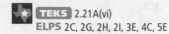 **TEKS** 2.21A(vi)
ELPS 2C, 2G, 2H, 2I, 3E, 4C, 5E

 **Draw a line from each noun to the pronoun that could replace it. Then tell a partner a story using the nouns and pronouns below.**

1. Dad and Mom   he

2. the girl   it

3. Grandpa   I

4. the TV   we

5. Shari and I   they

6. _____   she
    (write your first name here)

 In each sentence, write a pronoun to replace the noun. If you need help, check the list of pronouns on page 392 in *Write Source*.

1. _____ went to a movie.
    (Jim and Ray)

2. _____ broke his arm.
    (The boy)

3. A doctor fixed _____.
                 (the arm)

4. _____ is a good writer.
    (Jane)

TEKS 2.21A(vi)
ELPS 2C, 2G, 2H, 2I, 3E, 4C, 5E

Name _____

Pronouns 2

A **pronoun** can take the place of a possessive noun. A possessive noun shows ownership.

Noun	**Pronoun**
Jan's bicycle	her bicycle
Dave's skateboard	his skateboard
the bird's wing	its wing
Mike and Laura's poem	their poem

A Circle the pronouns that take the place of the underlined nouns in the sentences below. Then say sentences using the pronouns below.

1. Juanita's coat is red.

(Her) coat is hanging up.

2. At the picnic, Jake's lunch fell into the water.

His lunch was soggy.

3. Yesterday Sam and Sarah missed the bus.

Their bus left early.

4. The dog was very excited.

It chewed on a big bone.

TEKS 2.21A(vi)
ELPS 2C, 2G, 2H, 2I, 3E, 4C, 5E

B Underline the pronoun in each sentence. Draw a picture of the pet rat. Then discuss pets you know with a partner using pronouns.

1. Here is my pet rat.

2. Dad likes its pink ears.

3. Mom likes its long tail.

4. Bogart is our favorite pet.

5. He has red eyes.

6. Ted pets his white fur.

7. We bought a blue cage.

C Draw a line to the pronoun that could replace the underlined words.

1. I heard <u>Tim and Judy's</u> song.   ours

2. I know <u>your sister's</u> name.   Its

3. Here comes <u>Ricky's</u> friend.   their

4. <u>The book's</u> cover got wet.   his

5. The tree house is <u>yours and mine</u>.   her

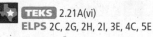 2.21A(vi)
ELPS 2C, 2G, 2H, 2I, 3E, 4C, 5E

131

Name _____

Pronouns 3

A **pronoun** is a word that takes the place of a noun.

Jason made a **sandwich.**
Then **he** ate **it.**
(The pronouns *he* and *it* take the place of the nouns *Jason* and *sandwich.*)

 Fill in each blank with a pronoun that replaces the underlined word or words. Then say a few sentences using the pronouns *they* and *we*.

1. Joe and Ann read a poem. ___They___ read it aloud.

2. Tanya drew a map. _____ showed it to me.

3. My brother and I have a clubhouse. _____ made

it ourselves.

4. I hope you're coming to my party. _____ will be fun.

5. Mom heard our music. _____ was too loud.

6. Tony is coming over. _____ is my friend.

7. The monkeys ate bananas. _____ were hungry.

8. This book is great. _____ has good pictures, too.

TEKS 2.21A(vi)
ELPS 2C, 2G, 2H, 2I, 3E, 4C, 5E

B Use each pronoun in a sentence.

I	we	she	they

1. _____

2. _____

3. _____

4. _____

C Draw a picture to go with one of your sentences. Discuss your picture with a partner using the pronoun in the sentence.

⭐ **ELPS** 2C, 2G, 2H, 2I, 3E, 4C

133

Name _____

Action Verbs

There are different kinds of **verbs**.
Some verbs show action:

Mom **found** our jump rope.
She **gave** it to us.

 **Underline the action verb in each sentence. Then choose one of the action verbs to use in your own sentence. Tell your sentence to a partner.**

1. Al <u>brings</u> the jump rope.

2. Eli and Linda hold the rope.

3. They twirl the rope.

4. The other kids count.

5. Scott's dog barks at the children.

6. Today Al jumps 100 times!

7. Then Linda takes a turn.

8. Mother waves from the window.

9. The kids laugh.

ELPS 4C

B Here are some more action verbs. Fill in each blank with a verb from this box.

dive	hear	pop
roars	visit	eat

1. Paul and Ann _____ the zoo.

2. They _____ some lions.

3. One of the lions _____ at them.

4. The elephants _____ lots of peanuts.

5. The polar bears _____ into the pool.

6. Prairie dogs _____ out of their tunnels.

Write a sentence about the zoo. Use an action verb.

_____

_____

_____

ELPS 2C, 4C

Name _____

Action and Linking Verbs

Action verbs show action. Here are some examples:

kick   tell   throw   ask   run   write

Linking verbs complete a thought or an idea. Here are some examples:

am   was   is   were   are   be

A   Write **A** if the underlined verb is an action verb. Write **L** if the verb is a linking verb.

___A___ **1.** Soccer players <u>kick</u> the ball.

_____ **2.** Football players <u>throw</u> the ball.

_____ **3.** I <u>am</u> cold.

_____ **4.** Pat and Rob <u>run</u> around the track.

_____ **5.** She <u>is</u> a fast runner.

_____ **6.** They <u>are</u> both in second grade.

_____ **7.** He <u>paints</u> pictures.

_____ **8.** Pete and Joni <u>were</u> sick.

ELPS 4C

B Pick five action verbs from the list on page 511 in *Write Source*. Use each action verb in a sentence.

1. _____

_____

2. _____

_____

3. _____

_____

4. _____

_____

5. _____

_____

Write a sentence using the linking verb *am*.

_____

_____

Name _____

Verbs: Present and Past Tense

A verb that tells what is happening now is called a **present-tense verb**.

Sean **is** in second grade.

He **takes** swimming lessons every week.

A verb that tells what happened in the past is called a **past-tense verb**.

Last year he **was** in first grade.

He **learned** to play soccer.

 Check whether each underlined verb is in the present tense or the past tense.

	Present Tense	Past Tense
1. Bobby <u>broke</u> his leg last weekend.	____	✓
2. He <u>fell</u> out of a big tree.	____	____
3. Now he <u>has</u> a cast on his leg.	____	____
4. He <u>is</u> home from school this week.	____	____
5. Yesterday I <u>took</u> him his homework.	____	____
6. I <u>wrote</u> my name on his cast.	____	____

TEKS 2.21A(i)
ELPS 2C, 2G, 2H, 2I, 3E, 4C, 5E

B Complete the following sentences. Write the present-tense verb or the past-tense verb in the blank. The first one has been done for you.

Present Tense

1. Now Mom ___makes___ my lunches for school.
(makes, made)

2. Now I _____ eight years old.
(am, was)

3. The sidewalk _____ slippery when it snows.
(gets, got)

4. Now Stanis _____ swimming lessons.
(takes, took)

Past Tense

1. Last week I _____ to school with Hector.
(walk, walked)

2. Yesterday Lydia _____ a letter to her aunt.
(write, wrote)

3. Last summer our family _____ camping.
(goes, went)

4. This morning I _____ late for school.
(am, was)

TEKS 2.21A(i)
ELPS 2C, 2G, 2H, 2I, 3E, 4C, 5E

Name _____

Verbs: Present and Future Tense

A verb that tells what will happen in the future is called a **future-tense** verb.

We **will be** in third grade next year.

 A Write the future tense for each verb. Then add two of your own examples. Tell a partner a sentence using one of the future-tense verbs.

1. climbed   *will climb*

2. make   _____

3. gct   _____

4. carry   _____

5. wanted   _____

6. play   _____

7. _____

8. _____

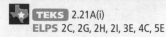 **TEKS** 2.21A(i)
ELPS 2C, 2G, 2H, 2I, 3E, 4C, 5E

 **B** **Fill in the blanks by changing the present-tense word under the line into the future tense.**

Next summer we _____ all the way across
                (drive)

West Texas. We _____ in my hometown of Austin.
           (start)

We _____ only the big highways. First, we
     (take)

_____ overnight in Fort Stockton where Grandma
(stay)

lives. Then we _____ up early the next day. We
           (wake)

_____ driving until we reach El Paso, the western
(keep)

tip of Texas.

Tell a partner what you will do over your next vacation. Use the future tense.

TEKS 2.21A(i)
ELPS 2C, 2G, 2H, 2I, 3E, 4C, 5E

Name _____

Irregular Verbs

Irregular verbs do not follow the same rules as other verbs. They change in different ways.

Present tense	Past tense
Example: Birds fly.	Birds flew.

Study the irregular verbs in your textbook. Then complete the exercise below.

 A Circle the correct verb in each sentence. Then tell a partner a sentence using one of the irregular verbs below.

1. My friend Kara ((rode,) ridden) a pony.

2. Uncle Billy (came, come) to visit us.

3. Last night, I (sung, sang) with my cousin.

4. Alfonso (saw, seen) a moose at the zoo.

5. Oscar (done, did) a good job on his art project.

6. The pitcher (threw, throw) the ball to first base.

142

TEKS 2.21A(i)
ELPS 2C, 2G, 2H, 2I, 3E, 4C, 5E

B In the sentences below, fill in the blank with the correct form of the verb shown. Then tell a partner sentences using the verbs *go* and *went.*

1. was   am

present: I _____ taking dance lessons.

past: I started dancing when I _____ four.

2. hide   hid

present: Sometimes, I _____ from my dog.

past: Yesterday, I _____ from him.

3. ran   run

present: We _____ with my big brother.

past: Last week, we _____ at the track.

4. knew   know

present: I _____ Olivia.

past: When we met, I _____ we would be friends.

TEKS 2.21A(iii)
ELPS 2C, 2G, 2H, 2I, 3B, 3E, 4C

Name _____

Adjectives 1

An **adjective** describes a noun or a pronoun. An adjective often comes before the word it describes.

Megan has long hair.
Randy wears a black cap.

Sometimes an **adjective** comes after the word it describes.

Parrots are colorful.

A **Underline the adjective that describes each circled noun. Then tell a partner about an animal. Use at least two adjectives.**

1. Elephants are huge (animals.)

2. Their (skin) is wrinkled.

3. Their ivory (tusks) are long (teeth.)

4. Elephants use their floppy (ears) as giant (fans.)

5. An elephant's trunk works as a useful (tool.)

6. It can pick up small (peanuts.)

7. A cool (river) is an elephant's favorite (place.)

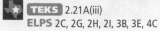
TEKS 2.21A(iii)
ELPS 2C, 2G, 2H, 2I, 3B, 3E, 4C

B Fill in each blank with an adjective that describes the circled noun.

1. Elephants make _____ (noises.)

2. Elephants have _____ (trunks.)

3. They have _____ (feet.)

4. Elephants can carry _____ (loads.)

5. Would you take a _____ (ride) on an

elephant?

6. How would you get on a _____ (elephant?)

C Underline each adjective that describes the circled pronoun. Then tell a partner a sentence using the adjective *silly*.

1. (You) are smart.

2. (He) is funny.

3. (They) look tired.

4. (I) am hungry.

5. (It) is green.

6. (We) are cold.

7. (She) feels sick.

8. (They) taste stale.

TEKS 2.21A(iii)
ELPS 2C, 2G, 2H, 2I, 3B, 3E, 4C

Name _____

Adjectives 2

An **adjective** describes a noun or a pronoun. An adjective often comes before the word it describes.

The hungry bear sniffed the berries.

Sometimes an **adjective** comes after the word it describes.

The bear was hungry.

 A **Underline the adjectives in this story. There are 12 in all. (Don't underline *a* or *that*.) Then add a sentence to the story using adjectives. Tell your sentence to a partner.**

Once there was a little brown bear.

In the cool forest, she ate crunchy roots and red berries.

On summer days, the bear ate and ate.

In the fall, little bear changed.

She was a great, big bear.

She crawled into a cozy den for a long winter nap.

★ TEKS 2.21A(iii)
ELPS 2C, 2G, 2H, 2I, 3B, 3E, 4C

B Write one more sentence for the story about the little bear. Underline the adjectives you use.

_____

_____

C Write two sentences using adjectives from the box below. Try using more than one adjective in your sentences. Then choose another adjective from the box and speak using it in a sentence.

hairy	purple	loud	cold
windy	wet	sweet	soft
chewy	sleepy	strong	sour

1. _____

_____

2. _____

_____

TEKS 2.21A(iii)
ELPS 2C, 2G, 2H, 2I, 3B, 3E, 4C

Name _____

Articles

The words *a*, *an*, and *the* are articles.

Use *a* before a consonant sound.

↗ a kit*e*

Use *an* before a vowel sound.

↗ an ocean

A Write *a* or *an* before the following words. Then tell a sentence a partner using *a* or *an*.

__an__ **1.** attic   _____ **9.** whale

_____ **2.** chicken   _____ **10.** shadow

_____ **3.** shovel   _____ **11.** envelope

_____ **4.** elephant   _____ **12.** idea

_____ **5.** tooth   _____ **13.** monkey

_____ **6.** giant   _____ **14.** orange

_____ **7.** dinosaur   _____ **15.** package

_____ **8.** apple   _____ **16.** kettle

★ TEKS 2.21A(iii)
ELPS 2C, 2G, 2H, 2I, 3B, 3E, 4C

B Fill in the word *a* or *an* in the spaces below.

One day _____ spider with yellow feet climbed

to the top of _____ slide. The slide was in _____

park. Soon the spider heard _____ radio playing her

favorite song. The song was _____ old tune called

"The Eensy Weensy Spider." The spider began to tap her

eight yellow feet. _____ inchworm heard the music,

too. He inched his way over to the slide and began to tap

all of his feet. What _____ funny sight to see!

_____ spider and _____ inchworm were dancing in

the park.

**Draw a picture of the spider and
the inchworm. Discuss your picture with a
partner using the words *a* or *an*.**

TEKS 2.21A(iii)
ELPS 2C, 2G, 2H, 2I, 3B, 3E, 4C

Name _____

Adjectives That Compare

Adjectives use different word endings to make comparisons. The ending *-er* compares two people, places or things. The ending *-est* compares three or more.

Compare **two**:

> My brother's room is small**er** than my room.

Compare **three or more**:

> The baby's room is the small**est** room in our house.

A **Fill in each blank with the correct form of the adjective. Then tell a partner three sentences using the words *easier* and *easiest*.**

longer, longest

1. A boa is _____ than a grass snake.

2. A python is the _____ snake in the zoo.

funnier, funniest

1. Leah's riddle was _____ than Garrett's riddle.

2. Ty's riddle was the _____ one in class.

150

TEKS 2.21A(iii)
ELPS 2C, 2G, 2H, 2I, 3B, 3E, 4C

B Circle the adjective that compares two people, places, or things. Underline the adjective that compares three or more.

1. Kenny is the tallest player on the team.

2. Silver Lake is deeper than Cross Creek.

C Write one sentence using the adjective below. Then, tell a partner another sentence using the adjective *happiest*.

bigger

_____

_____

TEKS 2.21A(iv)
ELPS 2C, 2G, 2H, 2I, 3E, 4C

Name _____

Adverbs 1

An **adverb** is a word that describes a verb. It tells *when*, *where*, or *how* an action is done.

Some adverbs tell **when:**
   yesterday   soon   always   early

Some adverbs tell **where:**
   here   inside   up   below

Some adverbs tell **how:**
   quietly   carefully   loudly   quickly

A   **In each sentence below, circle the adverb that tells *when*. Then tell a partner a sentence using a *when* adverb.**

1. Aldo has never seen snow.

2. We woke up early so we could go fishing.

3. Tomorrow, our class is going to the museum.

4. Salma always wears her hair in braids.

TEKS 2.21A(iv)
ELPS 2C, 2G, 2H, 2I, 3E, 4C

 In each sentence below, fill in the blank with an adverb that tells *where*.

1. Our teacher will be _____ tomorrow.

2. Do you want to play _____ this afternoon?

3. I saw a mouse run _____ the stairs!

 Fill in each blank with an adverb from the box below. These adverb tells *how*.

gently	**quickly**	**softly**	**cheerfully**

1. Alexis smiled _____ when she won the race.

2. "Have you seen Cory?" I asked _____.

3. Malik danced _____ as he sang.

4. I rocked my baby sister _____.

Tell a partner about a great day you had using when, where, and how adverbs.

TEKS 2.21A(iv)
ELPS 2C, 2G, 2H, 2I, 3E, 4C

Name _____

Adverbs 2

An **adverb** is a word that describes a verb. It tells *when*, *where*, or *how* an action is done.

Some adverbs tell **when**:
finally   tomorrow

Some adverbs tell **where**:
under   over

Some adverbs tell **how**:
slowly   softly

A Use adverbs to fill in each list below.

When	Where	How
1. yesterday	1. _____	1. _____
2. _____	2. _____	2. _____
3. _____	3. _____	3. _____

B Use your lists to tell a partner about a time you tried something new.

TEKS 2.21A(iv)
ELPS 2C, 2G, 2H, 2I, 3E, 4C

C Fill in each blank with an adverb from the box.

quickly	carefully	in
quietly	often	under

1. Animals in the woods are _____ busy.

2. Squirrels look for acorns _____ fallen leaves.

3. Deer _____ munch on weeds and grass.

4. Raccoons _____ open nuts for snacks.

5. Owls _____ watch for their prey.

6. Birds sing from high _____ the trees.

Choose two words from the box above. Use the words to tell a partner about an animal you have seen.

TEKS 2.21A(v)
ELPS 2C, 2G, 2H, 2I, 3E, 4C

Name _____

Prepositions

A **preposition** is used to add information to a sentence.

Toby hit the ball **over** the fence.

Ally put a quarter **in** her bank.

Here are some common prepositions.

onto	up	with	at	of
before	below	like	in	to
as	over	down	along	on

A Circle the prepositions in the paragraph below. The chart above will help you. Tell a partner what happens to Troy next using prepositions.

1. Troy left camp (before) breakfast. 2. He pushed his bike to the top of the hill. 3. Soon, he was racing down it. 4. The wind rushed through his hair. 5. The bike's wheels bumped along the grassy path. 6. "Woo-hoo!" Troy shouted with joy.

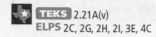 TEKS 2.21A(v)
ELPS 2C, 2G, 2H, 2I, 3E, 4C

 **Use the prepositions in this box to complete the following sentences. You will use one of the prepositions twice.**

like	of	in	above	until

1. Beluga whales live _____ cold, Arctic waters.

2. Belugas are gray _____ they become adults.

3. Then they turn white _____ their parents.

4. They are often called "sea canaries" because

_____ their songs and chatter.

5. Belugas swim _____ groups called pods.

6. Their sounds can be heard _____ the water.

 Tell a partner a sentence using a preposition from the box above.

TEKS 2.21A(v)
ELPS 2C, 2G, 2H, 2I, 3E, 4C

157

Name _____

Prepositions and Prepositional Phrases

A **preposition** is used to add information to a sentence.

I live **in** a blue house.

A **prepositional phrase** begins with a preposition.

I live **in a blue house.**

 A **Underline the prepositional phrases. Remember that they start with a preposition. Then use prepositional phrases to tell a partner how to get to your house.**

1. It's easy to get <u>to my house</u>.

2. First, go toward the high school.

3. Then go over that new bridge.

4. Next go straight up a steep hill.

5. My house is near the post office.

6. There it is between two tan houses.

7. You will find me inside the blue house!

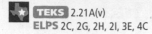

TEKS 2.21A(v)
ELPS 2C, 2G, 2H, 2I, 3E, 4C

B Choose a preposition to begin each prepositional phrase.

behind	onto	around	on
with	for	after	in

1. Do something nice _____ your dog.

2. Give your dog a bath _____ the tub.

3. Sprinkle water _____ your dog's fur.

4. Rub soap _____ the wet fur to make suds.

5. Wash all _____ the dog's body.

6. Don't forget to wash _____ your dog's ears.

7. Gently dry your dog _____ a towel.

8. Give your dog lots of love _____ the bath.

Use prepositional phrases to tell a partner how you clean your bedroom.

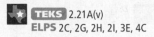
 **Write a preposition to begin each prepositional phrase.**

1. We have fun playing any time _____ the year.

2. Most often we play _____ the playground.

3. In spring, we fly kites up _____ the hill.

4. In the summer, we swim _____ the lake.

5. Sometimes we read books _____ a tree.

6. During the fall, we rake leaves _____ the yard.

7. When its cold in winter, we play _____ the house.

8. Mostly, we just like to play _____ our friends.

Tell a partner what you enjoy doing in each season. Use prepositional phrases.

ELPS 2C, 3C, 4C, 5F

Name _____

Conjunctions

A **conjunction** connects words or groups of words. The words *and* and *but* are the most common conjunctions.

Ramon writes poems **and** sings songs.

I was on time, **but** Tom wasn't there.

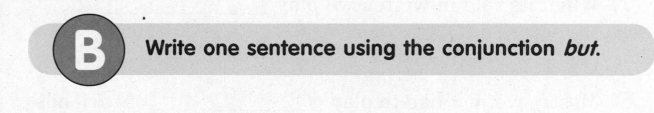

A   Write one sentence using the conjunction *and.*

_____

_____

B   Write one sentence using the conjunction *but.*

_____

_____

Two other conjunctions that connect words or groups of words are *or* and *so*.

Is Todd **or** Jaimee ready to bat?

It looked like rain, **so** she brought an umbrella.

C Circle the seven conjunctions in the story below.

The Tortoise and the Hare

Who won the race, the tortoise or the hare? They started out together, but the hare was much faster. He was way ahead of the tortoise, so he took a nap. The hare was snoring and dreaming when the tortoise walked by. Soon, the hare woke up, and he was amazed at what he saw. The tortoise was near the finish line! The hare ran to catch up, but it was too late. The tortoise won the race.

D Write a sentence using the conjunction *or*.

_____

ELPS 2C, 4C

Name _____

Interjections

An **interjection** shows excitement.
Some common interjections are:

Wow!   Yum!   Help!

Ouch!   Oops!   Hey!

A Write interjections to complete these sentences.

1. _____ ! This soup tastes delicious.

2. _____ ! I dropped my slice of pizza.

3. _____ ! I'm falling off the swing.

B Write a sentence using one of the interjections from above.

_____

_____

C Draw a picture for each sentence below. Label each picture with an interjection.

_____

(interjection)

Look what I can do.

_____

(interjection)

That bug is huge.

_____

(interjection)

I pinched my finger!

_____

(interjection)

I dropped my lunch tray.

Name _____

Parts of Speech Review 1

In this activity, you will review the parts of speech you have practiced: **noun (N)**, **pronoun (P)**, **verb (V)**, and **adjective (A)**.

A What part of speech is underlined in each sentence? Write **N**, **P**, **V**, or **A** in the blank.

_____ **1.** I like <u>toasted</u> cheese sandwiches.

_____ **2.** They <u>smell</u> buttery and <u>look</u> golden brown.

_____ **3.** When I <u>bite</u> into one, I <u>see</u> the melted cheese.

_____ **4.** Toasted cheese <u>sandwiches</u> taste crunchy on the outside and creamy in the middle.

_____ **5.** <u>My</u> mom makes them on the griddle.

_____ **6.** <u>I</u> could eat one every day!

_____ **7.** I hope we have toasted cheese sandwiches for <u>dinner</u> tonight.

_____ **8.** It would be a <u>super</u> way to end my day.

Fill in the blanks below.

1. Write the name of your favorite food (noun):

_____

2. Write a word that describes it (adjective):

_____

C **Fill in each blank with a word that is the correct part of speech.**

1. _____ likes tuna sandwiches.
 (noun)

2. _____ like tacos bcttcr.
 (pronoun)

3. I _____ two tacos every day.
 (verb)

4. I like them with _____ cheese.
 (adjective)

5. Sandra's mom _____ the best tacos.
 (verb)

6. She puts _____ sauce on them.
 (adjective)

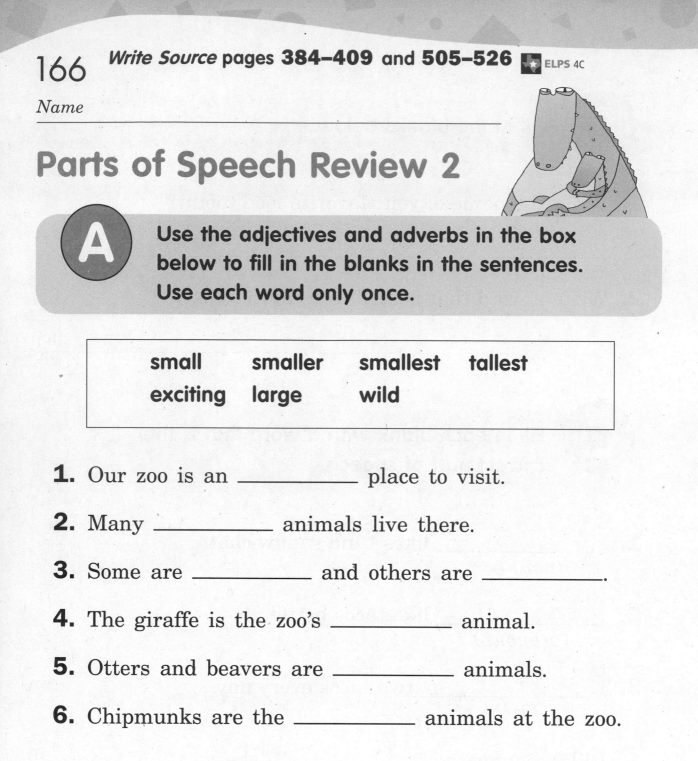

Name _____

Parts of Speech Review 2

A   Use the adjectives and adverbs in the box below to fill in the blanks in the sentences. Use each word only once.

small	smaller	smallest	tallest
exciting	large	wild	

1. Our zoo is an _____ place to visit.

2. Many _____ animals live there.

3. Some are _____ and others are _____ .

4. The giraffe is the zoo's _____ animal.

5. Otters and beavers are _____ animals.

6. Chipmunks are the _____ animals at the zoo.

Underline the prepositions in these sentences.

1. One cat rested on the desktop.

2. Another cat hid inside a drawer.

3. It hid under some papers.

 Use a comma and a conjunction to combine these short sentences. Use *or*, *and*, or *but*.

1. Should we play inside? Should we play outside?

_____

2. We went to the park. We had a picnic.

_____

 Write a sentence. Use one of the interjections below.

Wow!   **Yippee!**   **Help!**

_____

_____

Name _____

Parts of Speech
Review 3

 Choose the adverb that makes the most sense in each sentence.

1. Parrots squawk _____ in the treetops.
(loudly, calmly)

2. Monkeys swing _____ through the branches.
(easily, sadly)

3. Cheetahs run _____ behind their prey.
(softly, quickly)

4. Elephants walk _____ across the plain.
(heavily, gently)

5. Alligators slide _____ into the river.
(smoothly, gladly)

6. Snakes slither _____ through the grass.
(quietly, wildly)

 Underline each prepositional phrase in the sentences above.